Vegetarian Cookbook

The Ultimate Quick And Delicious Vegetarian Recipes For Healthy Lifestyle

Adrian Hess

VEGAN

GLUTEN FREE

FOOD

Adrian Hess

VEGETARIAN COOKBOOK

100% Vegetarian

Table of Contents

INTRODUCTION

Gradually introducing your body and palate to a vegetarian diet can help you adjust. The key is to take everything slowly. Start having Meatless Tuesdays, for example, then have one cheat day in a week. Little by little remove your meat from your diet, until such time that you can survive without them. Another tip is to let go of one animal product at a time. Doing away with all meat and dairy products in one go could lead you to hating vegetarianism. In essence, you will have to train yourself to "like" the diet, while you are getting rid of one animal product each week.

This is also an opportune time to get creative with your meals. Detractors may say that you are missing so much nutrients with a vegetarian diet, but that is not true. As long as you are getting protein, minerals, and other vitamins from a food source, a meatless diet wouldn't be much of a problem.

The vegetarian diet comes with many health benefits. For starters, it promotes weight loss. Vegetarian diets have also been looked as an effective way to decrease body mass index (BMI), which is crucial in maintaining a healthy body weight. On average, those transitioning to a vegetarian diet can lose about 2kg for 18 weeks, as compared to non-vegetarians. Those with type 2 diabetes might also find in losing weight more doable in the vegetarian diet as opposed to a general low-calorie diet.

If there is one drawback of the vegetarian diet, it's the sudden change in your temperament as you go through the transition period. Animal products leave a residue in your digestive system, which could lead you a bit depressed because it rigs your hormones. To help you detoxify gently, you can flush out toxins with lots of water. Squeeze in lemon juice from time to time for flavor and a kick of vitamin C.

On a more positive note, vegetarian diets can be good for the heart. Vegetarian diets can help decrease triglycerides levels and bad cholesterol in the bloodstream, which is why it is speculated that a vegetarian diet may soon trump the Mediterranean diet where heart health is concerned.

BREAKFAST

1. <u>CHEESY SQUASH BREAKFAST CASSEROLE</u>

Preparation Time: 10 minutes

Cooking Time: 25 minutes

Servings: 6

INGREDIENTS

- 12 organic eggs, beaten
- Salt and pepper
- 2 cups spaghetti squash, cooked
- 1 cup heavy cream
- 1 cup cheddar cheese, shredded
- ½ cup bell pepper, diced
- 4 tablespoons butter, melted

DIRECTIONS

1. Preheat your oven to 350°Fahrenheit. Take your baking dish and spray it with cooking spray and set aside.
2. In a mixing bowl, add all ingredients and mix well until combined.
3. Pour mixture into the prepared baking dish. In your preheated oven bake for 25 minutes or until done.
4. Allow cooling then you can serve and enjoy!

NUTRITION VALUES: Calories: 435 Fat: 37 g Carbohydrates: 5 g Sugar: 1.3 g Protein: 18.56 g Cholesterol: 395 mg

2. CHOCO BUTTER BREAKFAST SHAKE

Preparation Time: 10 minutes

Servings: 2

INGREDIENTS

- 2 tablespoons peanut butter, unsweetened

- 4 drops Stevia, liquid

- ½ cup coconut milk, unsweetened

- 2 scoops vanilla protein powder

- 2 tablespoons coconut oil

DIRECTIONS

1. Add all your ingredients into your blender and blend until smooth. Serve and enjoy!

NUTRITION VALUES: Calories: 467 Fat: 35 g Carbohydrates: 5.49 g Sugar: 3.1 g Protein: 30.45 g Cholesterol: 0 mg

ADRIAN HESS

CHOCO BUTTER BREAKFAST SHAKE

3. <u>SIMPLE BAKED EGG</u>

Preparation Time: 5 minutes

Cooking Time: 15 minutes

Servings: 1

INGREDIENTS

- 1 large organic egg
- Salt and pepper
- 1 tablespoon heavy cream
- 1 teaspoon parsley, chopped
- 1 teaspoon chives, chopped
- ½ teaspoon butter

DIRECTIONS

1. Preheat your oven to 350° Fahrenheit. Grease ramekin with ½ teaspoon of butter. Crack an egg into a greased ramekin. Add heavy cream over egg then sprinkle chopped chives, parsley, salt, and pepper on top. Place ramekin into the oven and bake for 15 minutes. Serve and enjoy!

NUTRITION VALUES: Calories: 173 Fat: 15.7 g Carbohydrates: 0.5 g Sugar: 0.4 g Protein: 6.4 g Cholesterol: 221 mg

ADRIAN HESS

SIMPLE
BAKED EGG

4. __CREAMY ORANGE BREAKFAST SHAKE__

Preparation Time: 10 minutes

Servings: 4

INGREDIENTS

- 1 teaspoon orange extract
- 1 cup ice cubes
- 8-ounces cream cheese
- 1 ¼ cups almond milk, unsweetened
- ¼ cups almond
- ¼ teaspoon Stevia, powder
- 1 teaspoon vanilla

DIRECTIONS

1. Add all your ingredients into your blender and blend until smooth. Serve and enjoy!

NUTRITION VALUES: Calories: 213 Fat: 20.6 g Carbohydrates: 2.1 g Sugar: 0.4 g Protein: 4.6 g Cholesterol: 62 mg

ADRIAN HESS

CREAMY ORANGE BREAKFAST SHAKE

5. <u>MINT ALMOND BREAKIE SHAKE</u>

Preparation Time: 10 minutes

Servings: 2

INGREDIENTS

- 2 teaspoons mint extract

- 1 cup ice cubes

- 1 cup vanilla almond milk, unsweetened

- 4-ounces cream cheese

- ½ cup mint leaves

- ½ teaspoon Stevia, liquid

DIRECTIONS

1. Add all your ingredients into your blender and blend until smooth. Serve and enjoy!

NUTRITION VALUES: Calories: 238 Fat: 21 g Carbohydrates: 4 g Sugar: 0.6 g Protein: 8.5 g Cholesterol: 62 mg

ADRIAN HESS

MINT ALMOND BREAKIE SHAKE

6. ENGLISH MUFFIN

Preparation Time: 10 minutes

Cooking Time: 1 minute

Servings: 1

INGREDIENTS

- 1 tablespoon Parmesan cheese, grated
- 1 teaspoon butter
- 1 large organic egg
- 2 teaspoons coconut flour
- 1/8 teaspoon baking soda
- 1/8 teaspoon sea salt

DIRECTIONS

1. Grease ramekin with butter and set aside. In a small bowl, combine egg and coconut flour. Now add all remaining ingredients, mix well. Place dough into prepared ramekin. Place ramekin into the microwave and microwave for I minute. Allow cooling for 5 minutes. Slice muffin in half and serve.

NUTRITION VALUES: Calories: 200 Fat: 14.3 g Carbohydrates: 4.4 g Sugar: 0.9 g Protein: 13.3 g Cholesterol: 206 mg

ADRIAN HESS

ENGLISH MUFFIN

7. __CHOCO BREAKFAST PUDDING__

Preparation Time: 10 minutes

Cooking Time: 5 minutes

Servings: 4

INGREDIENTS

- 1 teaspoon vanilla extract

- 1/8 teaspoon sea salt

- 2 cups full fat coconut milk, divided

- ½ cup cocoa powder, unsweetened

- 1 tablespoon powdered gelatin

- 1 cup almond milk, unsweetened

- ½ teaspoon Stevia powder

DIRECTIONS

1. Add gelatin and ¼ cup coconut milk in a mixing bowl, stir well and set aside. Add remaining coconut milk in a saucepan and heat for 5 minutes or until hot. Pour almond milk into microwave safe bowl and microwave for 1 minute. Add cocoa powder and stevia into gelatin and mix well. Pour almond milk and coconut milk into gelatin mixture and stir continuously. Add vanilla extract and salt. Pour batter into the four serving cups and place in fridge until they set. Serve and enjoy!

NUTRITIONAL VALUES (Per Serving): Calories: 392 Fat: 36 g Carbohydrates: 13 g Sugar: 5 g Protein: 10 g Cholesterol: 0 mg

MAINS

8. TOFU PESTO ZOODLES

Preparation Time: 5 minutes

Cooking Time: 12 minutes

Servings: 4

INGREDIENTS

- 2 tbsp olive oil
- 1 medium white onion, chopped
- 1 garlic clove, minced
- 2 (14 oz) blocks firm tofu, soaked and cubed
- 1 medium red bell pepper, deseeded and sliced
- 6 medium zucchinis, spiralized
- ¼ cup basil pesto, olive oil-based
- Salt and freshly ground black pepper to taste
- ½ cup shredded Gouda cheese
- 2/3 cup grated Parmesan cheese
- Toasted pine nuts to garnish

DIRECTIONS

1. Over medium fire, heat olive oil in a medium pot and sauté onion and garlic until softened and fragrant, 3 minutes.
2. Add tofu and cook until golden on all sides. Pour in bell pepper and cook until softened, 4 minutes.

17

3. Mix in zucchinis, pesto, salt, and black pepper. Cook for 3 minutes or until zucchinis soften slightly. Turn heat off and carefully mix in Gouda cheese to melt.

4. Dish into four plates, top with Parmesan cheese, pine nuts, and serve.

NUTRITION VALUES: Calories 477, Total Fat 32g, Total Carbs 12.04, Fiber 6.6g, Net Carbs 5.44g, Protein 20.42

9. CHEESY MUSHROOM PIE

Preparation Time: 10 minutes

Cooking Time: 43 minutes + 1 hour refrigeration

Servings: 4

INGREDIENTS

For piecrust:

- 3 tbsp coconut flour
- ¼ cup almond flour + extra for dusting
- ½ tsp salt
- ¼ cup butter, cold and crumbled
- 3 tbsp swerve sugar
- 1 ½ tsp vanilla extract
- 4 whole eggs, cracked into a bowl

For filling:

- 2 tbsp butter
- 1 medium brown onion
- 2 garlic cloves, minced
- 1 green bell pepper, deseeded and diced
- 1 cup green beans, cut into 3 pieces each
- 2 cups mixed mushrooms, chopped
- Salt and freshly ground black pepper to taste
- ¼ cup coconut cream
- 1/3 cup sour cream
- ½ cup unsweetened almond milk
- 2 eggs, lightly beaten

- ¼ tsp nutmeg powder
- 1 tbsp freshly chopped parsley
- 1 cup grated cheddar cheese

DIRECTIONS

For piecrust:

1. Preheat oven to 350°F and grease a pie pan with cooking spray. Set aside.
2. In a large bowl, combine coconut flour, almond flour, and salt.
3. Add butter and mix with an electric hand mixer until crumbly. Add swerve sugar, vanilla extract, and mix well. Pour in eggs one after another while mixing until formed into a ball.
4. Flatten dough on a chopping board, cover in plastic wrap, and refrigerate for 1 hour.
5. Lightly dust chopping board with almond flour, unwrap dough, and roll out into a large rectangle of ½-inch thickness. Fit dough in pie pan, and cover with parchment paper.
6. Pour in some baking beans and bake in oven until golden, 10 minutes. Remove after, pour out beans, remove parchment paper, and allow cooling.

For filling:

1. Meanwhile, melt butter in a skillet and sauté onion and garlic until softened and fragrant, 3 minutes. Add bell

pepper, green beans, mushroom, salt and black pepper; cook for 5 minutes.

2. In a medium bowl, beat coconut cream, sour cream, almond milk, and eggs. Season with salt, black pepper, and nutmeg. Stir in parsley and cheddar cheese.

3. Spread mushroom mixture in baked crust and top with cheese filling.

4. Bake until golden on top and cheese melted, 20 to 25 minutes.

5. Remove; allow cooling for 10 minutes, slice, and serve.

NUTRITION VALUES: Calories 527, Total Fat 43.58g, Total Carbs 8.73g, Fiber 2.2g, Net Carbs 6.53g, Protein 21.3g

10. MEATLESS FLORENTINE PIZZA

Preparation Time: 10 minutes

Cooking Time: 25 minutes

Servings: 2

INGREDIENTS

For pizza crust:

- 6 eggs
- 1 tsp Italian seasoning
- 1 cup shredded provolone cheese

For topping:

- 2/3 cup tomato sauce
- 2 cups baby spinach, wilted
- ½ cup grated mozzarella cheese
- 1 (7 oz) can sliced mushrooms, drained
- 4 eggs
- Olive oil for drizzling

DIRECTIONS

For pizza crust:

1. Preheat oven to 400° F and line a pizza pan with parchment paper. Set aside.
2. Crack eggs into a medium bowl and whisk in Italian seasoning and provolone cheese.
3. Spread mixture on pizza pan and bake until golden, 10 minutes. Remove and allow cooling for 2 minutes.

For pizza:

1. Increase oven's temperature to 450° F.

2. Spread tomato sauce on crust, top with spinach, mozzarella cheese, and mushrooms. Bake for 8 minutes.

3. Crack eggs on top and continue baking until eggs set, 2 minutes.

4. Remove, slice, and serve.

NUTRITION VALUES: Calories 646, Total Fat 39.19g, Total Carbs 8.42g, Fiber 3.5g, Net Carbs 4.92g, Protein 36.87g

11. MARGHERITA PIZZA WITH CAULIFLOWER CRUST

Preparation Time: 8 minutes

Cooking Time: 30 minutes

Servings: 2

INGREDIENTS

For pizza crust:

- 2 cups cauliflower rice
- 4 eggs
- ¼ cup shredded Monterey Jack cheese
- ¼ cup shredded Parmesan cheese
- ½ tsp Italian seasoning
- Salt and freshly ground black pepper to taste

For topping:

- 6 tbsp unsweetened tomato sauce
- 1 small red onion, thinly sliced
- 2 ½ oz cremini mushrooms, sliced
- 1 tsp dried oregano
- ½ cup cottage cheese
- ½ tbsp. olive oil
- A handful fresh basil

DIRECTIONS

For pizza crust:

1. Preheat oven to 400° F and line a baking sheet with parchment paper.

2. Pour cauliflower into a safe microwave bowl, sprinkle with 1 tablespoon of water, cover with plastic wrap and microwave for 1 to 2 minutes or until softened. Remove and allow cooling.

3. Pour cauliflower into a cheesecloth and squeeze out as much liquid. Transfer to a mixing bowl.

4. Crack in eggs, add cheeses, Italian seasoning, salt, and black pepper. Mix until well-combined.

5. Spread mixture on baking sheet and bake in oven until golden, 15 minutes.

6. Remove from oven and allow cooling for 2 minutes.

For topping:

1. Spread tomato sauce on pizza crust, scatter onion and mushrooms on top, sprinkle with oregano, and add cottage cheese. Drizzle with olive oil and bake until golden, 15 minutes.

2. Remove, top with basil, slice and serve.

NUTRITION VALUES: Calories 290, Total Fat 22.58g, Total Carbs 6.62g, Fiber 5.8g, Net Carbs 0.82g, Protein 12.81g

ADRIAN HESS

MARGHERITA PIZZA WITH CAULIFLOWER CRUST

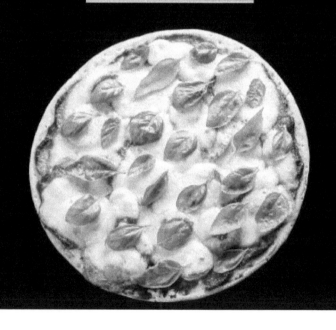

12.   **ALMOND TOFU LOAF**

Preparation Time: 10 minutes

Cooking Time: 1 hour

Servings: 4

INGREDIENTS

- 3 tbsp olive oil + extra for brushing
- 4 garlic cloves, minced
- 2 white onions, finely chopped
- 1 lb firm tofu, pressed and cubed
- 2 tbsp coconut aminos
- ¾ cup chopped almonds
- Salt and freshly ground black pepper
- 1 tbsp dried mixed herbs
- ½ tsp erythritol
- ¼ cup golden flax seed meal
- 1 tbsp sesame seeds
- 1 cup chopped mixed bell peppers
- ½ cup tomato sauce

DIRECTIONS

1. Preheat oven to 350∘F and lightly brush an 8 x 4 inch loaf pan with olive oil. Set aside.

2. In a medium bowl, combine olive oil, garlic, onion, tofu, coconut aminos, almonds, salt, black pepper, mixed herbs, erythritol, golden flax seed meal, sesame seeds, and bell peppers, and mix well.

3. Fit mixture in loaf pan, spread tomato sauce on top, and bake in oven for 45 minutes to 1 hour.

4. Remove pan and turn tofu loaf over onto a chopping board.

5. Slice and serve with garden green salad.

NUTRITION VALUES: Calories 432, Total Fat 31.38g, Total Carbs 8.74g, Fiber 6.2g, Net Carbs 2.54g, Protein 24.36g

13.   KALE AND MUSHROOM BIRYANI

Preparation Time: 15 minutes

Cooking Time: 46 minutes

Servings: 4

INGREDIENTS

- 6 cups cauli rice
- 2 tbsp water
- Salt and freshly ground black pepper
- 3 tbsp ghee
- 3 medium white onions, chopped
- 1 tsp ginger puree
- 1 tbsp turmeric powder + more for dusting
- 2 cups chopped tomatoes
- 1 red chili, finely chopped
- 1 tbsp tomato puree
- 1 cup sliced cremini mushrooms
- 1 cup diced paneer cheese
- 1 cup kale, chopped
- 1/3 cup water
- 1 cup plain yogurt
- ¼ cup chopped cilantro
- Olive oil for drizzling

DIRECTIONS

1. Preheat oven to 400° F.

2. Pour cauliflower rice into a safe microwave bowl, drizzle with water, cover with plastic wrap, and microwave for 1 minute or until softened. Remove and season with salt and black pepper. Set aside.

3. Melt ghee in a casserole pan and sauté onion, ginger, and turmeric powder. Cook until fragrant, 5 minutes.

4. Add tomatoes, red chili, and tomato puree; cook until tomatoes soften, 5 minutes.

5. Stir in mushrooms, paneer cheese, kale, and water; season with salt and black pepper and simmer until mushrooms soften, 10 minutes. Turn heat off and stir in yogurt.

6. Spoon half of stew into a bowl and set aside. Sprinkle half of cilantro on remaining stew in casserole pan, top with half of cauli rice, and dust with turmeric. Repeat layering a second time with remaining ingredients.

7. Drizzle with olive oil and bake until golden and crisp on top, 25 minutes.

8. Remove; allow cooling, and serve with coconut chutney.

NUTRITION VALUES: Calories 346, Total Fat 21.48g, Total Carbs 8.63g, Fiber 6.6g, Net Carbs 2.03g, Protein 16.01g

ADRIAN HESS

KALE AND MUSHROOM BIRYANI

14. MUSHROOM PIZZA BOWLS WITH AVOCADO & CILANTRO

Preparation Time: 15 minutes

Cooking Time: 17 minutes

Servings: 4

INGREDIENTS

- 1 ½ cups broccoli rice
- 2 tbsp water
- Olive oil for brushing
- 2 cups unsweetened pizza sauce
- 1 cup grated Gruyere cheese
- 1 cup grated mozzarella cheese
- 2 large tomatoes, chopped
- ½ cup sliced cremini mushrooms
- 1 small red onion, chopped
- 1 tsp dried basil
- Salt and freshly ground black pepper to taste
- 1 avocado, halved, pitted, and chopped
- ¼ cup chopped parsley

DIRECTIONS

1. Preheat oven to 400° F.
2. Pour broccoli rice into a safe microwave bowl, drizzle with water, and steam in microwave for 1 to 2 minutes. Remove, fluff with a fork, and set aside.

3. Lightly brush the inner parts of four medium ramekins with olive oil and spread in half of pizza sauce. Top with half of broccoli rice and half of cheeses.

4. In a bowl, combine tomatoes, mushrooms, onion, basil, salt, and black pepper. Spoon half of mixture into ramekins and top with half of cheeses. Repeat layering a second time making sure to finish off with cheeses.

5. Bake until cheese melts and golden on top, 15 minutes.

6. Remove ramekins and top with avocados and parsley.

7. Allow cooling for 3 minutes and serve.

NUTRITION VALUES: Calories 378, Total Fat 22.54g, Total Carbs 12.27g, Fiber 8.9g, Net Carbs 3.37g, Protein 20.68g

15. PISTACHIOS AND CHEESE STUFFED ZUCCHINIS

Preparation Time: 15 minutes

Cooking Time: 17 minutes

Servings: 4

INGREDIENTS

- 1 cup riced broccoli
- ¼ cup vegetable broth
- 4 medium zucchinis, halved
- 2 tbsp olive oil + more for drizzling
- 1 ¼ cup diced tomatoes
- 1 medium red onion, chopped
- ¼ cup pine nuts
- ¼ cup chopped pistachios
- 4 tbsp chopped parsley
- 1 tbsp smoked paprika
- 1 tbsp balsamic vinegar
- Salt and freshly ground black pepper to taste
- 1 cup grated Parmesan cheese

DIRECTIONS

1. Preheat oven to 350∘F.
2. Pour broccoli rice and vegetable broth in a medium pot and cook over medium heat until softened, 2 minutes. Turn heat off, fluff broccoli rice, and allow cooling.

3. Scoop flesh out of zucchini halves, chop pulp and set aside. Brush zucchini boats with some olive oil. Set aside.

4. In a medium bowl, combine broccoli rice, tomatoes, red onion, pine nuts, pistachios, parsley, paprika, balsamic vinegar, zucchini pulp, salt, and black pepper.

5. Spoon mixture into zucchini boats, drizzle with more olive oil, and cover top with Parmesan cheese.

6. Place filled zucchinis on a baking sheet and bake until cheese melts and is golden, 15 minutes.

7. Remove, allow cooling, and serve.

NUTRITION VALUES: Calories 330, Total Fat 28.12g, Total Carbs 10.62g, Fiber 5.4g, Net Carbs 5.22g, Protein 12.3g

16. SOY CHORIZO-ASPARAGUS BOWL

Preparation Time: 15 minutes

Cooking Time: 15 minutes

Servings: 4

INGREDIENTS

- 1 lb soy chorizo, cubed
- 1 lb asparagus, trimmed and halved
- 1 cup green beans, trimmed
- 1 cup chopped mixed bell peppers
- 2 red onions, cut into wedges
- 1 head medium broccoli, cut into florets
- 2 rosemary sprigs
- Salt and freshly ground black pepper to taste
- 4 tbsp olive oil
- 1 tbsp maple (sugar-free) syrup
- 1 lemon, juiced

DIRECTIONS

1. Preheat oven to 400° F.
2. On a baking tray, spread soy chorizo, asparagus, green beans, bell peppers, onions, broccoli, and rosemary. Season with salt, black pepper, and drizzle with olive oil and maple syrup. Rub spices into vegetables.
3. Bake until vegetables soften and light brown around the edges, 15 minutes.

4. Dish vegetables into serving bowls, drizzle with lemon juice, and serve warm.

NUTRITION VALUES: Calories 300, Total Fat 18.55g, Total Carbs 12.5g, Fiber 9.2g, Net Carbs 3.3g, Protein 14.87g

17. ANTIOXIDANT ZUCCHINI, LETTUCE AND RADICCHIO SALAD

Servings: 4

INGREDIENTS

- 4 boiled zucchini
- 1 large lettuce head
- 2 chopped celery stalk
- ½ c. chopped almonds
- 4 sliced radishes,
- Olive oil (extra virgin)
- 1 lemon juice
- 4 tbsps. Parmesan cheese
- Salt
- Pepper

DIRECTIONS

1. Wash and slice your zucchini.
2. Heat the water in a pot over the medium heat.
3. Add the zucchini, cover and cook for 3 to 6 minutes or until the squash is tender.
4. Transfer zucchini in colander and drain well.
5. In a large bowl place lettuce, celery, sliced radishes and chopped celery; toss to combine.
6. Pour olive oil, lemon juice and sprinkle with Parmesan cheese; toss.

7. Serve.

NUTRITION VALUES: Calories: 168.4 Fat: 11.16g Carbs: 6.45g Protein: 8.4g

18. BAKED PUMPKIN "SPAGHETTI" WITH HERBES DE PROVENCE

Servings: 6

INGREDIENTS

- 1 large pumpkin for spaghetti squash
- ½ c. grass-fed butter
- 3 tsps. Herbes de Provence
- 1 pressed garlic clove
- 1 chopped scallion
- 1 tsp. lemon juice
- 4 tbsps. Grated Parmesan
- Salt
- Black pepper

DIRECTIONS

1. Preheat the oven to 375F.
2. Wash the pumpkin and cut in half.
3. In a shallow baking dish, add two halves face down and cover with foil.
4. Bake for 1 - 1 1/2 hours.
5. Mix the butter with the herbs, onion, pressed garlic and the lemon juice until creamy.
6. When the pumpkin is cooked, remove the seeds and remove the pulp with a fork (this produces wonderful spaghetti-like threads.

7. Place the pumpkin "spaghetti" and season with salt and pepper to taste.

8. Pour with the butter/herb mixture, sprinkle with the Parmesan and serve immediately.

NUTRITION VALUES: Calories: 204.22 Fat: 17.72g Carbs: 7.17g Protein: 3.7g

19. CABBAGE, CAULIFLOWER, AND LEEK PUREE

Servings: 4

INGREDIENTS

- ½ medium cabbage head
- 1 leek
- 4 c. cauliflower florets
- 2 tbsps. Olive oil
- Chopped Parsley
- Salt
- Pepper

DIRECTIONS

1. Chop the vegetables and wash well.
2. Heat water in a big pot and place the vegetables; season with salt.
3. Bring to boil, reduce the heat, cover and cook it 15 -20 minutes, until the vegetables are soft.
4. Transfer vegetables in a blender or food processor and add the oil; blend until smooth.
5. Taste and adjust salt and pepper.
6. Decorate with chopped parsley (optional) and serve.

NUTRITION VALUES: Calories: 128.37 Fat: 7.23g Carbs: 7.05g Protein: 3.84g

20.   CHILLED AVOCADO AND ENDIVE SOUP

Servings: 3

INGREDIENTS

- 3 endives
- 2 chopped spring onions
- 1 diced avocado
- 1 c. Greek yogurt
- 1 tbsp. olive oil
- 1 chopped garlic clove
- 3 cardamom seeds
- 4 chopped mint leaves
- Salt

DIRECTIONS

1. Place all ingredients from the list in your high speed blender.
2. Blend until smooth and creamy.
3. Refrigerate for 2-3 hours and serve cold.

NUTRITION VALUES: Calories: 193.1 Fat: 14.69g Carbs: 7.99g Protein: 5.71g

ADRIAN HESS

CHILLED AVOCADO AND ENDIVE SOUP

21. CREAMY WATERCRESS LUNCH DIP

Servings: 2

INGREDIENTS

- ½ lb. watercress
- 1½ c. cottage cheese
- ¾ c. Mayonnaise (gluten-free, grain free)
- ½ c. chopped chives and parsley
- 3 tbsps. Lemon juice
- Kosher salt
- Black pepper

DIRECTIONS

1. Place all ingredients from the list (watercress, cottage cheese, Mayonnaise (gluten-free, grain free), chives and parsley, lemon juice and salt) in your fast-speed blender.
2. Blend on HIGH speed until smooth.
3. Refrigerate for 1-2 hours.
4. Serve.

NUTRITION VALUES: Calories:31963 Fat: 17.49g Carbs 9.13g Protein: 23.49g

ADRIAN HESS

CREAMY WATERCRESS LUNCH DIP

SIDES

22. MASHED BROCCOLI WITH ROASTED GARLIC

Preparation Time: 5 minutes

Cooking Time: 37 minutes

Servings: 4

INGREDIENTS

- ½ head garlic
- 1 to 2 tbsp of olive oil
- 1 large head broccoli, cut into florets
- Water for boiling, about 3 cups
- 1 tsp salt
- 4 oz. vegan butter
- ¼ tsp dried thyme
- Juice and zest of half a lemon
- 4 tbsp coconut cream
- 4 tbsp olive oil + extra for topping

DIRECTIONS

1. Preheat oven to 400 F.

2. Use a knife to cut a ¼ inch off the top of the garlic cloves, drizzle with the olive oil, and wrap in aluminum foil.

3. Place the wrapped garlic on a baking sheet and roast in the oven for 30 minutes or until the cloves are lightly browned and feel soft when pressed.

4. Remove and set aside when ready.

5. Pour the broccoli into a pot, add the water, and 1 teaspoon of salt. Bring the broccoli to boil over medium heat until tender, about 7 minutes. Then, drain the water and transfer the broccoli to a large bowl.

6. Add the vegan butter, thyme, lemon juice and zest, coconut cream, and olive oil. Use an immersion blender to puree the ingredients until smooth and nice.

7. Spoon the mash into serving bowls and garnish with some olive oil.

8. Serve with grilled eggplants.

NUTRITION VALUES: Calories: 376; Total Fat: 33g; Total Carbs: 8g; Fiber: 2g; Net Carbs: 6g; Protein: 11g

23.   KENTUCKY BAKED CAULIFLOWER WITH MASHED PARSNIPS

Preparation Time: 5 minutes

Cooking Time: 30 minutes

Servings: 6

INGREDIENTS

- ½ cup unsweetened almond milk
- ¼ cup coconut flour
- ¼ tsp cayenne pepper
- 1 tsp salt
- ½ cup almond breadcrumbs
- ½ cup shredded vegan cheese
- 30 oz. cauliflower florets
- Mashed Parsnip
- 1 lb medium sized parsnips, peeled and quartered
- 3 tbsp melted vegan butter
- A pinch nutmeg
- 1 tsp cumin powder
- 1 cup coconut cream
- Salt to taste
- Water for boiling
- 2 tbsp sesame oil

DIRECTIONS

For the baked cauliflower

1. Preheat the oven to 425 F and line a baking sheet with parchment paper.

2. In a small bowl, combine the almond milk, coconut flour, and cayenne pepper. In another bowl, mix the salt, breadcrumbs, and vegan cheese. Dip each cauliflower floret into the milk mixture, coating properly, and then into the cheese mixture.

3. Place the breaded cauliflower on the baking sheet and bake in the oven for 30 minutes, turning once after 15 minutes.

For the parsnip mash

1. Make slightly salted water in a saucepan and add the parsnips. Bring to boil over medium heat for 10 to 15 minutes or until the parsnips are fork tender. Drain the parsnips through a colander and transfer to a bowl.

2. Add the melted vegan butter, cumin powder, nutmeg, and coconut cream. Puree the ingredients using an immersion blender until smooth.

3. Spoon the parsnip mash into serving plates and drizzle with some sesame oil. Serve with the baked cauliflower when ready.

NUTRITION VALUES: Calories: 385; Total Fat: 35g; Total Carbs: 12g; Fiber: 4g; Net Carbs: 8g; Protein: 6g

24. BUTTERED CARROT NOODLES WITH KALE

Preparation Time: 5 minutes

Cooking Time: 10 minutes

Servings: 4

INGREDIENTS

- 2 large carrots
- ¼ cup vegetable broth
- 4 tbsp vegan butter
- 1 garlic clove, minced
- 1 cup chopped kale
- ¼ tsp salt
- ¼ tsp freshly ground black pepper

DIRECTIONS

1. Peel the carrots with a slicer and run both through a spiralizer to form noodles.

2. Pour the vegetable broth into a saucepan and add the carrot noodles. Simmer (over low heat) the carrots for 3 minutes. Strain through a colander and set the vegetables aside.

3. Place a large skillet over medium heat and melt the vegan butter. Add the garlic and sauté until softened and put in the kale; cook until wilted.

4. Pour the carrots into the pan, season with the salt and black pepper, and stir-fry for 3 to 4 minutes.

5. Spoon the vegetables into a bowl and serve with pan-grilled tofu.

NUTRITION VALUES: Calories: 335; Total Fat: 28g; Total Carbs: 14g; Fiber: 6g; Net Carbs: 8g; Protein: 6g

25. BAKED SPICY EGGPLANT

Preparation Time: 5 minutes

Cooking Time: 25 minutes

Servings: 4

INGREDIENTS

- 2 large eggplants
- Salt and freshly ground black pepper
- 2 tbsp vegan butter
- 1 tsp red chili flakes
- 4 oz. raw ground almonds

DIRECTIONS

1. Preheat the oven to 400 F.

2. Cut off the head of the eggplants and slice the body into 2-inch rounds. Season with salt and black pepper and arrange on a parchment paper-lined baking sheet.

3. Drop thin slices of the vegan butter on each eggplant slice, sprinkle with red chili flakes, and bake in the oven for 20 minutes.

4. Slide the baking sheet out and sprinkle with the almonds. Roast further for 5 minutes or until golden brown. Dish the eggplants and serve with arugula salad.

NUTRITION VALUES: Calories: 230; Total Fat: 16g; Total Carbs: 8g; Fiber: 4g; Net Carbs: 4g; Protein: 14g

ADRIAN HESS

BAKED SPICY EGGPLANT

26.   SPICY PISTACHIO DIP

Preparation Time: 5 minutes

Servings: 4

INGREDIENTS

- 3 oz. toasted pistachios + a little for garnishing
- 3 tbsp coconut cream
- ¼ cup water
- Juice of half a lemon
- ½ tsp smoked paprika
- Cayenne pepper to taste
- ½ tsp salt
- ½ cup olive oil

DIRECTIONS

1. Pour the pistachios, coconut cream, water, lemon juice, paprika, cayenne pepper, and salt. Puree the ingredients on high speed until smooth.

2. Add the olive oil and puree a little further. Manage the consistency of the dip by adding more oil or water.

3. Spoon the dip into little bowls, garnish with some pistachios, and serve with julienned celery and carrots.

NUTRITION VALUES: Calories: 220; Total Fat: 19g; Total Carbs: 7g; Fiber: 2g; Net Carbs: 5g; Protein: 6g

27. PARMESAN CROUTONS WITH ROSEMARY TOMATO SOUP

Preparation Time: 10 minutes

Cooking Time: 1 hour 15 minutes

Servings: 6

INGREDIENTS

Parmesan Croutons:

- 3 tbsp flax seed powder + 9 tbsp water
- 1¼ cups almond flour
- 2 tsp baking powder
- 5 tbsp psyllium husk powder
- 1 tsp salt
- 1¼ cups boiling water
- 2 tsp plain vinegar
- Olive oil for greasing

Parmesan topping

- 3 oz. vegan butter
- 2 oz. grated vegan parmesan cheese
- Rosemary Tomato Soup
- 2 lb fresh ripe tomatoes
- 4 cloves garlic, peeled only
- 1 small white onion, diced
- 1 small red bell pepper, seeded and diced

- 3 tbsp olive oil
- 1 cup coconut cream
- ½ tsp dried rosemary
- ½ tsp dried oregano
- 2 tbsp chopped fresh basil
- Salt and freshly ground black pepper to taste
- Basil leaves to garnish

DIRECTIONS

For the parmesan croutons:

1. In a medium bowl, mix the flax seed powder with 2/3 cup of water and set aside to soak for 5 minutes. Preheat the oven to 350 F and line a baking sheet with parchment paper.

2. In another bowl, combine the almond flour, baking powder, psyllium husk powder, and salt.

3. When the flax egg is ready, mix in the boiling water and plain vinegar. Then, add the flour mixture and whisk for 30 seconds just to be well combined but not overly mixed.

4. Grease your hands with some olive oil and form 8 flat pieces out of the dough. Place the flattened dough on the baking sheet while leaving enough room between each to allow rising. Bake the dough for 40 minutes or until crispy.

5. Remove the croutons to cool and break them into halves.

6. Mix the vegan butter with vegan parmesan cheese and spread the mixture in the inner parts of the croutons.

7. Increase the oven's temperature to 450 F and bake the croutons further for 5 minutes or until golden brown and crispier.

For the tomato soup:

1. In a baking pan, add the tomatoes, garlic, onion, red bell pepper, and drizzle with the olive oil.

2. Roast the vegetables in the oven for 25 minutes and after broil for 3 to 4 minutes until some of the tomatoes are slightly charred.

3. Transfer the vegetables to a blender and add the coconut cream, rosemary, oregano, basil, salt, and black pepper. Puree the ingredients on high speed until smooth and creamy. If the soup is too thick, add a little water to lighten the texture.

4. 1Pour the soup into serving bowls, drop some croutons on top, garnish with some basil leaves, and serve.

NUTRITION VALUES: Calories: 434; Total Fat: 38g; Total Carbs: 12g; Fiber: 6g; Net Carbs: 6g; Protein: 11g

28.   PAPRIKA ROASTED NUTS

Preparation Time: 3 minutes

Cooking Time: 7 minutes

Servings: 4

INGREDIENTS

- 8 oz. walnuts and pecans
- 1 tsp salt
- 1 tbsp coconut oil
- 1 tsp cumin powder
- 1 tsp paprika powder

DIRECTIONS

1. In a bowl, mix the walnuts, pecans, salt, coconut oil, cumin powder, and paprika powder until the nuts are well coated with spice and oil.

2. Pour the mixture into a frying pan and toast over medium heat while stirring continually.

3. Once the nuts are fragrant and brown, transfer to a bowl. Allow to cool and serve with a chilled berry juice.

NUTRITION VALUES: Calories: 290; Total Fat: 27g; Total Carbs: 6g; Fiber: 3g; Net Carbs: 3g; Protein: 6g

ADRIAN HESS

PAPRIKA ROASTED NUTS

29. SPINACH CHIPS WITH GUACAMOLE HUMMUS

Preparation Time: 12 minutes

Cooking Time: 15 minutes

Servings: 4

INGREDIENTS

Spinach Chips:

- ½ cup baby spinach
- 1 tbsp olive oil
- ½ tsp plain vinegar
- Salt to taste

Guacamole Hummus:

- 3 large avocados, ripe and soft
- ½ cup freshly chopped parsley + extra for garnishing
- ½ cup vegan butter
- ¼ cup pumpkin seeds
- ¼ cup sesame paste
- Juice from ½ lemon
- 1 garlic clove, minced
- ½ tsp coriander powder
- Salt and black pepper to taste

DIRECTIONS

Spinach Chips:

1. Preheat the oven to 300 F.

2. Rinse the spinach under running water and pat dry with a paper towel(s). Put the spinach in a bowl and toss with olive oil, plain vinegar, and salt.

3. After, arrange the spinach on a parchment paper-lined baking sheet and bake in the oven until the leaves are crispy but not burned, about 15 minutes. Toss a few times to ensure an even bake.

Guacamole Hummus:

1. Use a knife to cut the avocado in half lengthwise, take out the pit, and scoop the flesh into the bowl of a food processor.

2. Add the parsley, vegan butter, pumpkin seeds, sesame paste, lemon juice, garlic, coriander powder, salt, and black pepper. Puree the ingredients until smooth. If too thick, mix in some more olive oil or water. Spoon the hummus into a bowl and garnish with some parsley.

3. Serve the guacamole hummus with the spinach chips.

NUTRITION VALUES: Calories: 473; Total Fat: 45g; Total Carbs: 8g; Fiber: 5g; Net Carbs: 3g; Protein: 8g

VEGETABLES

30. STUFFED POBLANOS

Preparation Time: 50 minutes

Servings: 4

INGREDIENTS

- 2 tsp. garlic; minced
- 1 white onion; chopped
- 10 poblano peppers; one side of them sliced and reserved
- 1 tbsp. olive oil
- Cooking spray
- 8 oz. mushrooms; chopped
- A pinch of sea salt
- Black pepper to the taste
- 1/2 Cup Cilantro; Chopped

DIRECTIONS

1. Place poblano boats in a baking dish which you've sprayed with some cooking spray.
2. Heat up a pan with the oil over medium high heat, add chopped poblano pieces, onion and mushrooms, stir and cook for 5 minutes.
3. Add garlic, cilantro, salt and black pepper, stir and cook for 2 minutes.

4. Divide this into poblano boats, introduce them in the oven at 375 °F and bake for 30 minutes. Divide between plates and serve.

NUTRITION VALUES: Calories: 150; Fat: 3g; Fiber: 2g; Carbs: 4g; Protein: 10g

31. **TOMATO QUICHE**

Preparation Time: 30 minutes

Servings: 2

INGREDIENTS

- 1 bunch basil; chopped
- 4 eggs
- 1 garlic clove; minced
- A pinch of sea salt
- Black pepper to the taste
- 1/2 cup cherry tomatoes; halved
- 1/4 Cup Almond Cheese

DIRECTIONS

1. In a bowl; mix eggs with a pinch of sea salt, black pepper, almond cheese and basil and whisk well.
2. Pour this into a baking dish, arrange tomatoes on top, place in the oven at 350 °F and bake for 20 minutes. Leave quiche to cool down, slice and serve.

NUTRITION VALUES: Calories: 140; Fat: 1g; Fiber: 1g; Carbs: 2g; Protein: 10g

32. <u>LIVER STUFFED PEPPERS</u>

Preparation Time: 25 minutes

Servings: 4

INGREDIENTS

- 4 bacon slices; chopped
- 1 white onion; chopped
- 1/2 lb. chicken livers; chopped
- 4 garlic cloves; chopped
- 4 bell peppers; tops cut off and seeds removed
- A pinch of sea salt
- Black pepper to the taste
- 1/2 tsp. lemon zest; grated
- 1/4 tsp. thyme; chopped
- 1/4 tsp. dill; chopped
- A drizzle of olive oil
- A Handful Parsley; Chopped

DIRECTIONS

1. Heat up a pan over medium heat, add bacon, stir and cook for 2 minutes.
2. Add onion and garlic, stir and cook for 2 minutes.
3. Add livers, a pinch of salt and black pepper, stir; cook for 5 minutes and take off heat.
4. Transfer this to your food processor, blend very well, transfer to a bowl and aside for 10 minutes.

5. Add thyme, oil, parsley, lemon zest and dill, stir well and Stuff each bell pepper with this mix. Serve right away.

NUTRITION VALUES: Calories: 150; Fat: 3g; Fiber: 2g; Carbs: 5g; Protein: 12g

33. STUFFED PORTOBELLO MUSHROOMS

Preparation Time: 30 minutes

Servings: 4

INGREDIENTS

- 10 basil leaves
- 1 cup baby spinach
- 3 garlic cloves; chopped
- 1 cup almonds; roughly chopped
- 1 tbsp. parsley
- 2 tbsp. Nutritional yeast
- 1/4 cup olive oil
- 8 cherry tomatoes; halved
- A pinch of sea salt
- Black pepper to the taste
- 4 Portobello Mushrooms; Stem Removed and Chopped

DIRECTIONS

1. In your food processor, mix basil with spinach, garlic, almonds, parsley, Nutritional yeast, oil, a pinch of salt, black pepper to the taste and mushroom stems and blend well.

2. Stuff each mushroom with this mix, place them on a lined baking sheet, place in the oven at 400 °F and bake for 20 minutes. Divide between plates and serve right away.

NUTRITION VALUES: Calories: 145; Fat: 3g; Fiber: 2g; Carbs: 6g; Protein: 17g

34. ZUCCHINI NOODLES AND PESTO

Preparation Time: 20 minutes

Servings: 4

INGREDIENTS

- 6 zucchinis; trimmed and cut with a spiralizer
- 1 cup basil
- 1 avocado; pitted and peeled
- A pinch of sea salt
- Black pepper to the taste
- 3 garlic cloves; chopped
- 1/4 cup olive oil
- 2 tbsp. olive oil
- 1 lb. shrimp; peeled and deveined
- 1/4 cup pistachios
- 2 tbsp. lemon juice
- 2 Tsp. Old Bay Seasoning

DIRECTIONS

1. In a bowl; mix zucchini noodles with a pinch of sea salt and some black pepper, leave aside for 10 minutes and squeeze well.
2. In your food processor, mix pistachios with black pepper, basil, avocado, lemon juice and a pinch of salt and blend well.
3. Add 1/4 cup oil, blend again and leave aside for now.

4. Heat up a pan with 1 tbsp. oil over medium high heat, add garlic, stir and cook for 1 minute.

5. Add shrimp and old bay seasoning, stir; cook for 4 minutes and transfer to a bowl.

6. Heat up the same pan with the rest of the oil over medium high heat, add zucchini noodles, stir and cook for 3 minutes.

7. Divide on plates, add pesto on top and toss to coat well. top with shrimp and serve.

NUTRITION VALUES: Calories: 140; Fat: 1g; Fiber: 1g; Carbs: 5g; Protein: 14g

35. <u>SPAGHETTI SQUASH AND TOMATOES</u>

Preparation Time: 60 minutes

Servings: 4

INGREDIENTS

- 1/4 cup pine nuts
- 2 cups basil; chopped
- 1 spaghetti squash; halved lengthwise and seedless
- Black pepper to the taste
- A pinch of sea salt
- 1 tsp. garlic; minced
- 1½ tbsp. olive oil
- 1 cup mixed cherry tomatoes; halved
- 1/2 cup olive oil
- 2 Garlic Cloves; Minced

DIRECTIONS

1. Place spaghetti squash halves on a lined baking sheet, place in the oven at 375 °F and bake for 40 minutes.
2. Leave squash to cool down and make your spaghetti out of the flesh.
3. In your food processor, mix pine nuts with a pinch of salt, basil and 2 garlic cloves and blend well.
4. Add 1/2 cup olive oil, blend again well and transfer to a bowl.

5. Heat up a pan with 1½ tbsp. oil over medium high heat, add tomatoes, a pinch of salt, some black pepper and 1 tsp. garlic, stir and cook for 2 minutes. Divide spaghetti squash on plates, add tomatoes and the basil pesto on top.

NUTRITION VALUES: Calories: 150; Fat: 1g; Fiber: 2g; Carbs: 4g; Protein: 12g

36. DAIKON ROLLS

Preparation Time: 15 minutes

Servings: 4

INGREDIENTS

- 1/2 cup pumpkin seeds
- 2 green onions; chopped
- 1/2 bunch cilantro; roughly chopped
- 2 tbsp. avocado oil
- 1 tbsp. lime juice
- 2 tsp. water
- A pinch of sea salt
- Black pepper to the taste
- 2 daikon radishes; sliced lengthwise into long strips
- 1 small cucumber; cut into matchsticks
- 1/2 avocado; pitted, peeled and sliced
- Handful Microgreens

DIRECTIONS

1. In your food processor, mix pumpkin seeds with a pinch of sea salt, pepper, cilantro and green onions and blend very well.
2. Add avocado oil gradually and lime juice and blend very well again. Add water and blend some more.

3. Spread this on each daikon slice, add cucumber matchsticks, avocado slices and micro greens, roll them, seal edges, divide between plates and serve.

NUTRITION VALUES: Calories: 140; Fat: 0g; Carbs: 23g; Fiber: 0g; Protein: 0

37. <u>**GLAZED CARROTS**</u>

Preparation Time: 25 minutes

Servings: 4

INGREDIENTS

- 1 lb. carrots; sliced
- 1 tbsp. coconut oil
- 1 tbsp. ghee
- 1/2 cup pineapple juice
- 1 tsp. ginger; grated
- 1/2 tbsp. maple syrup
- 1/2 tsp. nutmeg
- 1 Tbsp. Parsley; Chopped

DIRECTIONS

1. Heat up a pan with the ghee and the oil over medium high heat, add ginger, stir and cook for 2 minutes.
2. Add carrots, stir and cook for 5 minutes.
3. Add pineapple juice, maple syrup and nutmeg, stir and cook for 5 minutes more. Add parsley, stir; cook for 3 minutes, divide between plates and serve.

NUTRITION VALUES: Calories: 100; Fat: 0.5g; Fiber: 1g; Carbs: 3g; Protein: 7g

ADRIAN HESS

GLAZED CARROTS

38. CAULIFLOWER PIZZA

Preparation Time: 40 minutes

Servings: 6

INGREDIENTS

- 1½ cups mashed cauliflower
- A pinch of sea salt
- Black pepper to the taste
- 1/2 cup almond meal
- 1½ tbsp. flax seed; ground
- 2/3 cup water
- 1/2 tsp. oregano; dried
- 1/2 tsp. garlic powder
- Pizza sauce for serving
- Spinach leaves; chopped and already cooked for serving
- Mushrooms; Sliced And Cooked For Serving

DIRECTIONS

1. In a bowl; mix flax seed with water and stir well.
2. In a bowl; mix cauliflower with almond meal, flax seed mix, a pinch of sea salt, pepper, oregano and garlic powder, stir well, shape small pizza crusts, spread them on a lined baking sheet and bake them in the oven at 420 °F and bake for 15 minutes.
3. Take pizzas out of the oven, spread pizza sauce, spinach and mushrooms on them, introduce in the oven again

and bake 10 more minutes. Divide between plates and serve.

NUTRITION VALUES: Calories: 150; Fat: 8g; Carbs: 20g; Fiber: 1g; Protein: 9g

39. <u>CUCUMBER WRAPS</u>

Preparation Time: 40 minutes

Servings: 4

INGREDIENTS

For the mayo:

- 1 tbsp. coconut aminos
- 3 tbsp. lemon juice
- 1 cup macadamia nuts
- 1 tbsp. agave
- 1 tsp. caraway seeds
- 1/3 cup dill; chopped
- A pinch of sea salt
- Some Water

For the filling:

- 1 cup alfalfa sprouts
- 1 red bell pepper; cut into thin strips
- 2 carrots; cut into thin matchsticks
- 1 cucumber; cut into thin matchsticks
- 1 cup pea shoots
- 4 Paleo Coconut Wrappers

DIRECTIONS

1. Put macadamia nuts in a bowl; add water to cover, leave aside for 30 minutes and drain well.

2. In your food processor, mix nuts with coconut aminos, lemon juice, agave, caraway seeds, a pinch of salt and dill and blend very well.

3. Add some water and blend again until you obtain a smooth mayo.

4. Divide alfalfa sprouts, bell pepper, carrot, cucumber and pea shoots on each coconut wrappers, spread dill mayo over them, wrap, cut each in half and serve.

NUTRITION VALUES: Calories: 140; Fat: 3g; Fiber: 3g; Carbs: 5g; Protein: 12g

1. Meanwhile; heat up a pan over medium high heat, add bacon and fry for a couple of minutes.

2. Add onion and beef and some black pepper, stir and cook for 7-8 minutes more.

3. Take carrots out of the oven, add them to the beef and bacon mix, stir and cook for 10 minutes. Sprinkle scallions on top, divide between plates and serve.

NUTRITION VALUES: Calories: 160; Fat: 2g; Fiber: 1g; Carbs: 2g; Protein: 12g

SALADS

40. CURRIED CAULIFLOWER SALAD

Preparation Time: 10 minutes

 Cooking Time: 5

Servings: 4

NUTRITIONAL VALUES: Calories: 165 Fat: 14 g. Protein: 3 g. Carbs: 9 g.

INGREDIENTS

- 300 grams Cauliflower, chopped into florets
- 100 grams Cherry Tomatoes
- 150 grams Red Bell Pepper, diced
- 50 grams White Onions, diced
- handful of Fresh Cilantro for garnish

For the Dressing:

- 1/4 cup Olive Oil
- 1 tbsp Lime Juice
- ½ tsp Turmeric Powder
- 1 tbsp Garam Masala
- 2 Green Chilis, minced
- Salt, to taste

DIRECTIONS

1. Blanch cauliflowers in boiling water for 3 minutes. Drain and allow to cool.

2. Whisk all ingredients for the dressing in a bowl. Toss in cauliflower, tomatoes, peppers, and onions.

3. Top with fresh cilantro.

41. ASIAN SLAW AND EDAMAME SALAD

Preparation Time: 5 minutes

Servings: 4

NUTRITIONAL VALUES: Calories: 190 Fat: 16 g. Protein: 3 g. Carbs: 9 g.

INGREDIENTS

- 50 grams Edamame
- 150 grams Carrots, cut into thin strips
- 150 grams Jicama, cut into thin strips
- 1 tbsp Sesame Seeds

For the Dressing:

- 3 tbsp Olive Oil
- 1 tbsp Sesame Oil
- 1 tbsp Tamari
- 1 tbsp Peanut Butter
- 1 tbsp Lime Juice
- 2 Red Chilis, minced
- 1 tbsp Erythritol

DIRECTIONS

1. Whisk all ingredients for the dressing in a bowl.

2. Toss in edamame, carrots, and jicama.

42. <u>FALAFEL SALAD</u>

Preparation Time: 10 minutes

Servings: 4

NUTRITIONAL VALUES: Calories: 143 Fat: 11 g. Protein: 3 g. Carbs: 9 g.

INGREDIENTS

- 300 grams Romaine Lettuce, chopped
- 50 grams Chickpeas
- 100 grams Tomatoes, diced
- 50 grams Shallots, thinly sliced
- Fresh Parsley for garnish

For the Dressing:

- ¼ cup Vegennaise
- 1 tsp Garlic Powder
- 1 tbsp Lemon Juice
- 1 tsp Cumin Powder
- ¼ tsp Salt

DIRECTIONS

1. Whisk together all ingredients for the dressing in a bowl.
2. Toss in lettuce, chickpeas, shallots, and tomatoes.
3. Top with chopped fresh parsley.

ADRIAN HESS

FALAFEL SALAD

43. ASIAN AVOCADO SALAD

Preparation Time: 4 hours

Servings: 4

NUTRITIONAL VALUES: Calories: 298 Fat: 29 g. Protein: 3 g. Carbs: 9 g.

INGREDIENTS

- 2 Avocados, peeled and diced
- 1 tbsp Sesame Seeds

For the Dressing:

- ¼ cup Sesame Oil
- 2 tbsp Lime Juice
  - tbsp Tamari
- 1 tbsp Minced Shallots
- 2 Red Chilis, minced
- 1 tbsp Erythritol

DIRECTIONS

1. Whisk all ingredients for the dressing in a bowl.
2. Toss in avocado and top with sesame seeds.

ADRIAN HESS

✕

ASIAN AVOCADO SALAD

SNACKS& DESSERT

44. BUFFALO TOFU PINWHEELS

Preparation Time: 20 minutes

Servings: 45 pinwheels

INGREDIENTS

- 3 green onions thinly sliced
- 6-oz. light cream cheese softened
- ½ cup Frank's Red-hot sauce
- 8-oz. sliced tofu medallions
- 4-6 strips of bread shaped like thin logs

DIRECTIONS

1. Mix your tofu with your cream cheese, green onions, and hot sauce until well blended.

2. Spread the buffalo tofu on the bread thin logs and roll them up like a jelly roll. Cut into ½ inch slices, place them in the fridge to chill.

3. Garnish with some sliced green onions.

ADRIAN HESS

BUFFALO TOFU PINWHEELS

45. <u>VEGETARIAN COCONUT LIME NOODLES</u>

Preparation Time: 35 minutes

Servings: 4

INGREDIENTS

- ½ tsp ground or fresh grated ginger
- 1 can full fat coconut milk
- 4 tbsp sesame seeds
- 2 packages of shirataki noodles
- Juice and zest of 1 lime

Optional:

- Red pepper flakes
- Salt

DIRECTIONS

1. Drain and rinse your noodles and place them in a pot over a temperature of medium heat, adding in the ingredients listed above. Mix them well to combine all the ingredients.
2. Next, place a lid on the pot, partially covering the pot, and cook the noodles for 10 minutes.
3. Next, lower your heat to low, continuing to cook for an additional 10 minutes.
4. Once your noodles are done, garnish them with whatever vegetables or tofu you would like to add to them.

ADRIAN HESS

VEGETARIAN COCONUT LIME NOODLES

46. SWEET AND SOUR CUCUMBER NOODLES WITH SOBA

Preparation Time: 35 minutes

Servings: 4

INGREDIENTS

- 2-3 Cucumbers medium
- 2 tsp. Honey
- ½ cup Rice Vinegar
- 4-oz. Soba Noodles
- 1 tbsp. Soy sauce

Optional:

- Green onions
- Sriracha sauce
- Hot sauce
- Sesame seeds
- Sambal olek

DIRECTIONS

1. Cook your Soba in some boiling water for only 5 minutes. They should be undercooked. Once done, drain them and rinse.

2. Combine your noodles with soy sauce and set them aside.

3. Now using a julienne peeler, thinly slice the cucumbers so that they are noodle-like.

4. Next, in a large bowl, add in your rice vinegar and honey, whisking till blended well.

5. Now, coat your cucumber noodles with the dressing and chill for 30 minutes.

6. Blend the soba with the cucumber and serve!

47. __FRIED GOAT CHEESE__

Preparation Time: 30 minutes

Servings: 2

INGREDIENTS

- 2 tbsp poppy seeds
- 2 tbsp sesame seeds
- 1 tsp onion flakes
- 4 -oz. goat cheese cut into ½ inch thick medallions
- 1 tsp garlic flakes

DIRECTIONS

1. Cut the goat cheese into ½ inch thick medallions.
2. Place the poppy seeds, garlic, onion, and sesame seeds in a bowl and mix well.
3. Place the goat cheese into the bowl individually and coat each side with seasoning.
4. Using a skillet with some olive oil for non-sticking, heat the pan to medium heat.
5. Fry the goat cheese on each side, making sure they do not fully melt.
6. Place on a plate for serving.

ADRIAN HESS

FRIED GOAT CHEESE

48. ORANGE MINT JALAPENO SALAD

Preparation Time: 10 minutes

Servings: 4

INGREDIENTS

- 10 assorted oranges
- Olive oil
- ¼ cup pine nuts
- 2 tbsp chopped jalapeno
- 1 handful of fresh mint leaves finely chopped

Optional: Sea salt

DIRECTIONS

1. Heat a small pan to a temperature of medium heat and sauté the pine nuts until golden brown. This should be about 2 minutes. They should be fragrant.
2. Place them on a cutting board using a knife to cut the ends off the oranges and slice the skin off. Cutting each orange into slices discard the orange seeds.
3. Arrange your slices on a plate and top it with chopped mint, jalapeno and pine nuts. Sprinkle with salt if you like and drizzle with olive oil for taste.
4. Serve immediately.

ADRIAN HESS

ORANGE MINT JALAPENO SALAD

49. BROCCOLI SALAD

Preparation Time: 15 minutes

Servings: 1-2

INGREDIENTS

- ½ cup shredded carrots
- ¼ cup raw sunflower seeds
- ½ cup red onions
- 1 head of broccoli cut into bite size pieces

Optional:

- ¼ cup raisins
- Sea salt
- Pepper

DIRECTIONS

1. In a bowl, add in the carrots, broccoli, red onion, sunflower seeds, and raisins if you like. Use any dressing that you like or the one mentioned below and toss it until the ingredients are evenly coated.
2. Serve and enjoy!

ADRIAN HESS

BROCCOLI SALAD

50. RHUBARB AND STRAWBERRY DESSERT

Preparation time: 10 minutes

Cooking time: 10 minutes

Servings: 4

INGREDIENTS

- 1/3 cup water
- 2 pound rhubarb, roughly chopped
- 3 tablespoons stevia
- 1 pound strawberries, halved
- A few mint leaves, chopped

DIRECTIONS

1. In your instant pot, mix water with rhubarb, stevia and strawberries, stir a bit, cover and cook on High for 10 minutes.
2. Add mint, stir, leave aside compote for a few minutes, divide into cups and serve.
3. Enjoy!

NUTRITION VALUES: Calories 100, Fat 2, Fiber 2, Carbs 3, Protein 2

CONCLUSION

Thanks for reading this guide. It is likewise important for you to have a goal. One goal is enough. Several short-term goals may also work for you – anything doable will do. Set realistic goals for yourself and stick to them. For instance, would you want to be vegetarian for only a week? Or would you want to have a one-month trial period? It is advisable that you don't do anything drastic, as it's so easy to backslide and lose the drive. It would also help to decide on the type of vegetarian you want to be.

As a beginner to vegetarianism, you may be tempted to purchase ready-to-eat meals, which companies claim as vegetarian. Most of these meals have been prepared with a set of calories in mind. You may choose to just have these meals delivered, though they may get expensive in the long run. Thus, maintaining this lifestyle depends on how much you are willing to spend. Should you buy your meals, choose a good vegetarian restaurant.

Another option is to research on various vegetarian recipes. Many are available online, and they have been prepared by chefs and food experts. Meanwhile, expand your search by adding a certain cuisine. Look for Japanese vegetarian recipes, Chinese, Mediterranean, or Middle Eastern.

Though risky, you may also up your ante and invent your recipes. You may substitute vegetables and fruits for variation. For example, you could have oatmeal with bananas on Monday, then oatmeal mixed with whole grain cereal and blueberries on Tuesday.

Lightning Source UK Ltd.
Milton Keynes UK
UKHW020651160421
382097UK00012B/739

9 781802 359282